Embracing Your Humanity

Before You Create

a

Business

Family

or an

Algorithm

That Fundamental Rite-of-Passage

Presented by
DALVA EVETTE YARRINGTON

A Mapped Experience

Embracing Your Humanity
Before Your Create a Business, Family or an Algorithm
That Fundamental Rite-of-Passage

© 2018 Dalva Evette Yarrington
Author
Human Development Experience Designer
Information and Data Scientist

ISBN-13: 978-1720349082
ISBN:1720349088

Introduction

This volume is a tool. If you have not encountered one of the previous iterations of this well-mapped experience you are in luck because you have this workbook in your hands. Filling-in your "blanks" is important. To convince yourself before you go any further, write down why you think a person should know who they are.

1. ____

2. ____

3. ____

It does not matter what you call this experience. I have called it a dozen different titles over the course of my lecturing and writing about it. Just call it fundamental, because it has fundamental relevance to every human being on this planet and living in this time. Time however does not make it more or less important. Your ability or opportunity to access information and to glean a deep empowering experience can be impacted by time and with age. All living creatures and plants take and carry something of an imprint from previous generations or iterations. That is because of original design and intent. Original design and intent are powerful and to demonstrate that, take a look at your own actions and your own family genealogy and heritage. This important transfer is unfortunately abbreviated or obfuscated in the times we now live.

We (many of us) have a handheld device which allows us access to databases containing important self-awareness and often no notion of how accessing this information early in life could enhance and underpin personal, community and group success. The distractions of unrelated persons and content have interfered with intergenerational self-awareness. It once was-- that ugly family secrets, abandonment or displacement were the worse threats to the sharing of self-knowledge. Today it may be the distracting device you have in your hand that is getting in the way of a conversation with your Elders. Self-knowledge is fundamental to self-awareness, to sustainable development and to mindfulness. There is no human civilization without it.

PREFACE

This is a ten-generation version of the TOUR MY ROOTS self-discovery map.

To begin, you should understand that new information requires time to settle into your psyche and resistance reminds you to check your sources and be an honest information broker.

A historical account should always be at least as accurate as you discovered it and your sources should be cited. Your "Aunt Viv" gets credit for telling you what your mother forgot to tell you or you failed to listen to.

When interviewing Elders be respectful and record with permission only! When the memory reservoirs of an Elder are opened, they do not close because you have to leave or end the conversation. Provide a means for them to land in a safe place mentally. They know a lot more than you've asked. They, The Elders are a powerful treasure whether you have recognized that fact or not! Happy and safe travels await, because you are well-mapped by TOUR MY ROOTS.

Everyone should have their own copy of this book to prepare their own unique history. The endless benefits begin with shared common data and evolves into an empowering and pivotal reality-check. I get chills every time I create another version of this tool, because I know how impactful this experience can be.

Your Index is on page 176. You cannot get lost. This is exactly how I would walk you through in a sociology or genealogy lecture or consultation. Start in the middle of each page with you or whomever is the "primary." Freedom and understanding await you. Family studies are not neat and tidy, but this experience can deliver a navigable and beneficial catharsis.

Embracing Your Humanity…

INSPIRED BY
GENESIS 10

DEDICATED

To Humanity… you sparkle in your details.

My Maternal Family
My Mother

The Human Ancestry
of

Start Date

My Paternal Family
My Father

This experience is important to me because…

My Mother's Birth

DOB

Time of Birth

Place of Birth

Delivered by

Birth Weight

Childhood Health Condition(s)

DOD

POD

Her Father

Her Mother

About My Birth

DOB

Time of Birth

Place of My Birth

My Birth Weight

Delivered by

My Childhood Health Condition(s)

My Father's Birth

DOB

Time of Birth

Place of Birth

Delivered by

Birth Weight

Childhood Health Condition(s)

DOD

POD

His Father

His Mother

More About My Birth

Rite-of-Passage

My Mother's Childhood

She Grew Up With

Her Maternal Birth Order

Her Paternal Birth Order

Her Primary Caregiver(s)/Nurturer(s)

My Mother Was Disciplined by

Places She Grew Up

My Childhood

I Grew Up With

My Maternal Birth Order

My Paternal Birth Order

My Caregivers

Places I Grew Up

My Father's Childhood

He Grew Up With

His Maternal Birth Order

His Paternal Birth Order

His Primary Caregiver(s)/Nurturer(s)

My Father Was Disciplined by

Places He Grew Up

More About My Mother's
Childhood Household

About My Childhood Household

Sources

More About My Father's
Childhood Household

Schools My Mother Attended

From - To

Schools I Attended | From - To

Schools My Father Attended

From - To

More About My Mother's Education

More About My Education

More About My Father's Education

My Mother's Occupations and Employers

My Occupations and Employers

My Father's Occupations and Employers

More About My Mother's Toils

More About My Work Life

More About My Father's Toils

My Mother's Achievements Timeline

My Achievements   Timeline

My Father's Achievements Timeline

Sources

My Mother's Memberships

My Memberships

My Father's Memberships

Rite-of-Passage

My Mother's Children

DOB

My Children

DOB

My Father's Children

DOB

More About My Mother's Children

More About My Children

More About My Father's Children

My Spouses and Childbearing Mates

More About My Mother's Mating

About My Mating

Sources

More About My Father's Mating

Rite-of-Passage

My Mother's Grandchildren

My Grandchildren

My Father's Grandchildren

More About My Mother's Grandchildren

More About My Grandchildren

More About My Father's Grandchildren

My Mother's Grandparents

Paternal Grandfather

Paternal Grandmother

Maternal Grandfather

Maternal Grandmother

My Grandparents

Paternal
Grandfather

Paternal
Grandmother

Maternal
Grandfather

Maternal
Grandmother

My Father's Grandparents

Paternal Grandfather

Paternal Grandmother

Maternal Grandfather

Maternal Grandmother

More About My Maternal Great Grandparents

More About My Grandparents

Sources

More About My Paternal Great Grandparents

Rite-of-Passage

Foreign Lands of My Mother's Family

Name	Place or Region

I was born in ____

At the time of My Birth my Country was being led by ___________

____

News of the Day I was born... _________________________

____

____

Foreign Lands of My Father's Family

Name	Place or Region

More About My Maternal Family Origins

More About My Place of Nativity

Population

Form of Governance

Peace, War, Famine etc...

Sources

More About My Paternal Family Origins

Foreign Languages of My Mother's Family	
Name	Language or Dialect

Languages Spoken in My Home

____

____

____

____

Foreign Languages of My Father's Family	
Name	Language or Dialect

About My Maternal Family

Languages I Speak

About My Paternal Family

Sources

Rite-of-Passage

Religious Traditions of My Mother's Family

Name	Religion

Religious Traditions in My Home

____

____

____

____

____

Religious Traditions of My Father's Family

Name	Religion

More About Maternal Religious Traditions

About My Rites-of-Passage

Sources

More About Paternal Religious Traditions

Rite-of-Passage

Name	Ethnicities
	28

Ethnicities in My Home

____

____

____

____

Ethnic Mixes in My Paternal Family

Name	Ethnicities

More About Ethnicity In My Maternal Family

More About Ethnicity and Culture In My Home

Sources

More About Ethnicity In My Paternal Family

Rite-of-Passage

About the Tools to Use

THE UNITED STATES CENSUS

This is a key source and should be used in its original form as a matter of course. Find your ancestors in each census taken during their lifetime. Take care to look at the neighbors as you will stumble upon absolutely fascinating details. That is a promise.

Be sure to read the tips and finding-aids of any online database. Archives go to great lengths to have you as informed as possible before granting you access to census records and other documents. Keep in mind that location boundaries have changed over time as well as the names of places. Be sure to research across state, county and municipal boundary lines in census data. A map of the region for the time of a specific census can save you great amounts of time, especially when an index for an enumeration is not available.

Be aware of spelling variations. One example: The midwife who delivered me Lucy [ ] Teate delivered over 350 babies in her career. She married a Louis Teate in Louisiana. If his Mississippi (Tate) family were looking for him in Louisiana, they would need to follow "see" references noted in some digital records pointing to the surname Teate. In the U. S. Census data I found the reuse of first names between the Tate and Teate families striking.

There are also just plain misspellings in both the official U.S. Census enumeration records and in the online transcriptions. One example is: My paternal family name was misspelled as "Yamington" in the 1880 U. S. Census transcription contained in the Familysearch.Org online database of the Church of Jesus Christ of Latter Day Saints. To find my paternal family in their 1880 census transcription, I had to know that in 1880 Great Grandma Anna Hays Yarrington was still living with her mother, my Great, Great Grandmother Ann Bland and where they were living. Ann Bland's name was spelled correctly. I had previously searched her name to find them in the microfilm files in 1985 at the Dallas Public Library. The same cautions about errors apply to other databases.

The great migration from the plantation to the plant influenced family clusters and in my estimation as dramatically as slavery had in the centuries before.

FAMILY MEMBERS WHO KEPT/KEEP RECORDS: ORAL AND OTHERWISE

The first rule here is to ask to take a digital picture of the information written in family Bibles, daybooks and ledgers. Ask to have the family photo albums digitally preserved. Make no mistake -information has great value. Be wary and insure against theft of your information, including paper and digital documents. If the de-facto family archivist refuses to allow you to digitize the collection of treasured family pictures, the best thing is to respect that refusal. The keeper probably knows the value and disrespecting their unwillingness to expose the family treasure will not serve you well later. It is important to make "the ask" clear, as a change of heart may occur. Tell your family member that you would like to do so, and wait until they consent or leave it as inheritance to someone who may be more willing to consent, or who will digitize it themselves and share a copy with you. Respect and diplomacy are paramount within and between family branches.

Many diaries and journals are in trunks and ship-a-robes and some contain jaw-dropping information. You might need an aspirin or night's sleep after some revelations.

Farmers often maintained detailed crop and transaction records, and sometimes meticulously because of mistrust of the local record-keepers. My maternal grandmother, Alberta (Babe) Meadows Jones kept a household and family event journal. The dollar amount for cotton income and cotton and soybean crop output information is listed by date as well as events such as graduations, baptisms and births. If she had kept a journal during the flood of 1927, it would have been the source for another book.   Most of that history was passed down orally. In Hoover's flood she walked for miles and miles carrying my aunt (age four at the time) to higher ground from Newlight to Gilbert, Louisiana slogging through the alligator clay. The most important thing for me is that her journal accounts are is in her own handwriting and my children, grandchildren and nieces will be able to see it and read it. Her journal also gave great insight into what she considered to be important, mentionable and keepsake information. I learned my first archival skills from my maternal grandparents. They used albums and lodge records to instruct me.

SLAVERY

Slavery was an enterprise and there are many ways to search for insights into slave breeding, cotton planting, harvesting and human trafficking.

1860 SLAVEHOLDER CENSUS
In 2004 when I created the first edition of my genealogy tools, published information giving the names of slaveholders and numbers of slaves held was almost non-existent. That has improved a bit.

It is possible to locate an ancestor on a U.S. Census for 1860 or earlier and not know that ancestor was also listed as a slaveholder on the slave schedules, because published indexes almost always do not include the slave census or a "see" reference to the Slaveholder Census. The last U.S. Census Slave Schedules were enumerated by County in 1860 and included 393,975 named persons holding 3,950,546 unnamed slaves, or an average of about ten slaves per holder. [ ] The names of those listed are slaveholders were some of the largest slaveholders in the listed County in 1860.

Keep in mind that the same systems which impacted Blacks-- also impacted Caucasians, Native Tribal groups and other somewhat distinct ethnic clusters. The outcomes were unique, but none-the-less impactful and breeding a common historic footprint. Sorting through these historic population patterns revealed that, we (humans all of one race) are often reluctant and slow learners from lessons illuminated in inspired texts and letters from thousands of years before. We keep hurting our COUSINS.

ADDITIONAL RESOURCES ON HUMAN SLAVERY MAY BE ACCESSED BY CONSULTING YOUR LOCAL LIBRARY PROFESSIONALS.

FAMILYSEARCH.ORG

This database has existed online in some version or another for some time. I have found it to be a most important change-agent in family history research and in access to genealogical data.

The Family Search database available online for some time was a transcription of the 1880 U.S. Census data and other records. Read the source notes and disclaimers. Use the search tips provided. You will also be able to click to a commercial link for a copy of actual census enumeration pages. I recommend that you get copies of important documentation, but I also recommend that you determine a satisfactory cost-benefit-ratio. The U. S. Census Data underpins what you find here. Some corresponding Canadian enumerations and some Social Security records are also searchable in the Familysearch.Org database.

There are information sharks-- waiting for you in the genealogy enterprise sector.

MARRIAGE BOOKS

Marriage books are a boon for many genealogists-- when they are made available.

From the transcribed and online marriage books in Tensas Parish, Louisiana, I was able to see that Richard (Dick) Jones [born a slave in Edwards, Mississippi] married Ora Bell [daughter of his Louisiana slaveholder and Justice-of-the-Peace] on January 1, 1869. I was also able to see that a person whose family became treasured cousins by marriage later, had stood-up at their wedding. By referencing the 1870 U. S. Census I could also link that person to another side of my family. In fact there was a Bass-Jones connection, a Bass-Meadows connection by labor and that same individual's descendants are connected today on all four sides of my family history.

My family reports Grandpa Dick was "A Tar-Black". Grandma Ora was the mulatto child of the mulatto slave Margaret Walters and the Caucasian plantation owner and Justice of the Peace William Bell of Tensas Parish. William Bell "purchased" Grandpa Dick when he was about 17 and before slavery ended from Dr. William S. Jones in Edwards, Mississippi. That was known from family oral history. Likely, from that same clan of Jones' that later populated the teaching community in the Mississippi River Delta. Grandpa Dick was determined that every one of his offspring knew that he (we) had people in Edwards, Mississippi. That is what it is reported that his mother told him to remember when he was sold away from her. No-doubt his maternal/paternal separation at age 17 caused all great anguish. That one marriage book excursion converging with family oral history brought to light a watershed of additional details. As a follow-up we asked questions of Aunt Alma Jones Bellows, the last living Jones to be rocked on the lap of that former slave.

The digital transcribers of marriage books and other county records have often been volunteers from local historical societies or social groups. You will find some errors, but much of the work is outstanding.

In the case of the books referenced above, Edith Ziegler was the able and generous transcriber. When you come across such generous work it is more than appropriate to send a thank you note whenever possible and always acknowledge transcribers in your narratives and compilations. Mind-you, some data collection and transcriptions are corrupted by oil and mineral greed and others by poorly informed transcribers. Original records are always preferable.

Many of these records are now scanned and that is significant as it removes or reduces the likelihood of secondary transcription errors.

NATIONAL ARCHIVES AND RECORDS ADMINISTRATION (NARA)

According to its website, NARA holds in trust over 5 billion pages of textual records; more than 14 million still pictures; about 300,000 reels of motion picture film; over 200,000 sound recordings; more than 15 million maps, charts, and aerial photographs; and over 170,000 electronic records files. The collections of NARA document the point where the lives of private citizens have intersected with the functions of the federal government. Census records, passenger lists, military service records, and land records can be found in the National Archives. The NARA website should be carefully consulted for further information on the scope of collections and on access. The National Archive and Records Administration "copies of records" can also be cost prohibitive for many. Cost comparison is appropriate. A trip to a regional branch of NARA can be useful when planned well. Having been the student of a former National Archivist (Dean Warner) I hold that standards were established and are hopefully currently being maintained.

BIRTH RECORDS

Birth records are collected at the county level and usually filed in duplicate at the state level. Many changes and upgrades have occurred in vital records management. Some were actually sound changes. Some states have very questionable standards in records management and access. In the aftermath of Hurricane Katrina many documents and vital paper records were at risk of loss.

You will need to check with the local county clerk for perhaps the best approach to a records search. Local civil servant archivists should share their wealth of tips with you when you request a consultative appointment. Experienced genealogist can be extraordinarily helpful in record and search queries for a price.

CHURCH RECORDS
Churches have always been a primary source for community records of various types. Check with the church personally to view, copy down or even be allowed to make a digital copy of event and circumstance information.

Never ask and never take Church or institutional documents out of the care of the custodian. Old documents should be handled with care and a fresh set of virgin cotton gloves is always appropriate, when allowed to handle important materials. Rare bookroom rules should be the norm when viewing one-of-a-kind, original and old treasured documents and artifacts.

DEATH RECORDS/ OBITUARIES

News reporting organizations (newspapers) are a rich source of reported deaths and events. They know that the information could be priceless, so ask up-front about fees and fashion your strategy accordingly. Even when cost is no object you should be careful of information access extortionist. Going to the library to search the newspapers on microfilm or fiche is likely cheaper. An obituary is often a family tree abstract and can offer clues on places lived, people married and work done as well as religious affiliations.

County governments are custodians of birth, death and tax data among other local government data sets. Be aware of fees and not afraid to question appropriateness of excesses.

The Passage Continues

Sources

People who kept and shared
Maternal History

Family History and Albums in My Home

People who kept and shared
Paternal History

Rite-of-Passage

About Maternal Documents and Records

Family Documents I Keep

Sources

About Paternal Documents and Records

Family Stories I Have Shared

Rite-of-Passage

More About Maternal Family Lore

More Family Lore

More About Paternal Family Lore

Sources

Sources

Maternal Family Connections To Fame

Name	Famous Connection

My Connection(s) To Fame

____

____

____

____

____

Paternal Family Connections To Fame

Name	Famous Connection

Rite-of-Passage

Sources

More About Maternal Fame and Infamy

About Fame and Infamy

More About Paternal Fame and Infamy

Maternal Connections to
Original Land Grants

Name	Location

About My Connections to Land

____

____

____

____

____

Paternal Connections to
Original Land Grants

Name	Location

Sources

Maternal Original Land Grant Descriptions

Inherited and Original Land Grant Assets

Sources

Paternal Original Land Grant Descriptions

Maternal Native or Indigenous Americans

Name	Tribe/Group…

My Known Native American Connection(s)

____

____

____

____

____

Paternal Native or Indigenous Americans

Name	Tribe/Group…

Sources

Rite-of-Passage

Sources

Dominant Maternal Cultural Identities

My Dominant Cultural Identity

Dominant Paternal Cultural Identities

My Maternal Grandmother's
Brothers and Sisters

My Mother's Aunts

My Mother's Uncles

My Maternal Grandmother had a Total of #_______ Children

My Maternal Grandfather Had a Total of #_______ Children

My Maternal Grandfather's
Brothers and Sisters

My Mother's Aunts

My Mother's Uncles

Sources

My Paternal Grandmother's
Brothers and Sisters

My Father's Uncles	My Father's Aunts

My Paternal Grandmother had a Total of #   Children

My Paternal Grandfather Had a Total of #   Children

My Paternal Grandfather's
Brothers and Sisters

My Father's Uncles	My Father's Aunts

Wealthy Maternal Family Members

Name	Description

Wealth in My Home

____

____

____

____

____

Wealthy Paternal Family Members

Name	Description

Sources

Rite-of-Passage

More About Maternal Wealth

About Generational Family Wealth

Sources

More About Paternal Wealth

Sources

Maternal Sharecroppers

Name	Location

My Cooperative Experiences

____

____

____

____

____

Paternal Sharecroppers

Name	Location

More About Maternal Agricultural Economics

Economic Disparities of My Lifetime

More About Paternal Agricultural Economics

Maternal Family Shopkeepers

Name	Location / Type

My Shopkeeping, Sales and Marketing Experiences

Paternal Family Shopkeepers

Name	Location / Type

More About Maternal Shopkeeping

More

More About Paternal Shopkeeping

Sources

Maternal Family Hoteliers and Innkeepers

Name	Location

Landlords. Innkeepers etc.

____

____

____

____

Paternal Family Hoteliers and Innkeepers

Name	Location

Rite-of-Passage

More About Maternal Landlords. Innkeepers etc.

More

Sources

More About Paternal Landlords. Innkeepers etc.

Sources

Maternal Farmers, Ranchers and Grocers

Name	Location

My Connection to Farming, Ranching and Grocery Chains

____

____

____

____

Paternal Farmers, Ranchers and Grocers

Name	Location

Rite-of-Passage

More About Agricultural Food
and Maternal Family Members

More about Agricultural Food and Me

Sources

More About Agricultural Food
and Paternal Family Members

Sources

Maternal Manufacturers, Designers and Crafters

Name	Product

Things I Make, Design or Craft

____

____

____

____

Paternal Manufacturers, Designers and Crafters

Name	Product

Rite-of-Passage

More About Maternal Family
Manufacturers, Designers and Crafters

More About Products I Make, Design or Craft

Sources

More About Paternal Family
Manufacturers, Designers and Crafters

Sources

Maternal Family Visual Artist and Art Dealers

Name	Describe

My Relationship with Visual Arts

Paternal Family Visual Artist and Art Dealers

Name	Describe

About My Maternal Family in the Arts Industry

More

Sources

About My Paternal Family in the Arts Industry

Maternal Family Elected and Appointed Officials

Name	Office/Location

My Elected and Appointed Positions

____

____

____

____

Paternal Family Elected and Appointed Officials

Name	Office/Location

More About My Maternal Family Officeholders

More about My Community, State and National Positions

Sources

More About My Paternal Family Officeholders

Maternal Family Military Service

Name	Branch/War/Dates

My Military Service

____

____

____

____

Paternal Family Military Service

Name	Branch/War/Dates

Sources

Rite-of-Passage

More About Maternal Military Service

More About My Service

More About Paternal Military Service

Sources

Maternal Family Preachers and Clergy

Name	Denomination and Location

My Relationship with Preaching and Religious Teaching

____

____

____

____

Paternal Family Preachers and Clergy

Name	Denomination and Location

More About Maternal Family Clergy

More About My Religious Calling and Training

Sources

More About Paternal Family Clergy

Maternal Family Tax Collectors and Undertakers

Name	Describe/Location

My Relationship With Tax Collecting and Undertaking

____

____

____

____

Paternal Family Tax Collectors and Undertakers

Name	Describe/Location

Sources

More About Maternal Family
Tax Collectors and Morticians

More About Tax Collecting and Undertaking

More About Paternal Family
Tax Collectors and Morticians

Maternal Family Bootleggers and etc.

Name	Product/Location

My Relationship with Home-Brewing

____

____

____

____

____

Sources

Paternal Family Bootleggers and etc.

Name	Product/Location

Rite-of-Passage

More About Maternal Family
Unlawful Enterprises

More Speaking Easy

More About Paternal Family
Unlawful Enterprises

Incarcerated Maternal Family Members

Name	Crime/ Location

My Relationship with Incarceration

____

____

____

____

____

Incarcerated Paternal Family Members

Name	Language or Dialect

More About Maternal Family Incarceration

More About Incarceration

More About Paternal Family Incarceration

Maternal Family Doctors, Nurses and Midwives

Name	Specialty/Location

My Relationship with Health Practitioners

____

____

____

____

____

Paternal Family Doctors, Nurses and Midwives

Name	Specialty/Location

More About Maternal Family
Health Practitioners

More About Health Care Practitioners in My Life

Sources

More About Paternal Family
Health Practitioners

Maternal Family Teachers, Authors Professors and Researchers

Name	Subject/Location

My Relationship with Teaching, Research and Education

____

____

____

____

Paternal Family Teachers, Authors Professors and Researchers

Name	Subject/Location

More About Maternal Family Educators

More About Teachers and Education in My Life

Sources

More About Paternal Family Educators

Maternal Family Engineers and Scientist

Name	Discipline/Industry

My Relationship with Engineering and Science

____

____

____

____

Paternal Family Engineers and Scientist

Name	Discipline/Industry

Sources

Sources

More About Maternal Family Engineers and Scientist

More About Engineers and Scientist in My Life

More About Paternal Family Engineers and Scientist

Maternal Family Cooks, Chefs and Bakers

Name	Areas of Expertise

My Food Skills

____

____

____

____

____

Paternal Family Cooks, Chefs and Bakers

Name	Areas of Expertise

More About My Food Skills

Sources

Sources

Maternal Family Construction Industry Workers

Name	Skill/Industry Area

My Relationship with Construction

____

____

____

Paternal Family Construction Industry Workers

Name	Skill/Industry Area

Rite-of-Passage

More About Maternal Family
Skilled Trade Workers

My Construction Skills

Sources

More About Paternal Family
Skilled Trade Workers

Sources

Maternal Family in Automotives and Mechanics

Name	Describe

My Relationship with Automobiles and Mechanics

____

____

____

____

Paternal Family in Automotives and Mechanics

Name	Describe

More About Maternal Family Auto Makers,
Dealers and Mechanics

More About Automobiles and My Life

More About Paternal Family Auto Makers,
Dealers and Mechanics

Sources

Maternal Family Bankers, Stock Traders and Insurance Agents

Name	Specify/Location

My Relationship with Bankers, Traders and Agents

____

____

____

____

Paternal Family Bankers, Stock Traders and Insurance Agents

Name	Specify/Location

Sources

More About Maternal Family Money Traders

More about the Financial Industry and My Life

More About Paternal Family Money Traders

Sources

Maternal Family Musical Artist or Managers

Name	Describe

My Relationship with the Music Industry

____

____

____

____

____

Paternal Family Musical Artist or Managers

Name	Describe

Rite-of-Passage

Sources

About My Maternal Family in the Music Industry

More

About My Paternal Family in the Music Industry

Sources

Maternal Family Athletes

Name	Sport/Team/Records

My Relationship with Sports and Athletics

____

____

____

____

Paternal Family Athletes

Name	Sport/Team/Records

More About Maternal Family Athletics

More about My Sports and Recreation

Sources

More About Paternal Family Athletics

Maternal Family Seamstresses, Tailors and Cobblers

Name	Specify/Describe

My Relationship with Sewing and Clothing Construction

____

____

____

____

Paternal Family Seamstresses, Tailors and Cobblers

Name	Specify/Describe

More About Maternal Family Clothing and Shoe Makers

More About Me Clothing and Shoemaking

More About Paternal Family Clothing and Shoe Makers

Maternal Family Logistics, Postal and Delivery Workers

Name	Service/Firm/Location

My Relationship with Logistics Work

____

____

____

____

Paternal Family Logistics, Postal and Delivery Workers

Name	Service/Firm/Location

Sources

Rite-of-Passage

More About Maternal Family
Distribution Workers

More About Logistics Workers

Sources

More About Paternal Family
Distribution Workers

Maternal Family Members Who Were Physically or Mentally Disadvantaged or Injured

Name	Describe

My Physical and Mental Challenges

Paternal Family Members Who Were Physically or Mentally Disadvantaged or Injured

Name	Describe

More About Maternal Disabilities

Physical and Mental Challenges I Have Overcome

Sources

More About Paternal Disabilities

Name	Age/Location

My Relationship with Abandonment

____

____

____

____

____

Name	Age/Location

Rite-of-Passage

More About Maternal
Abandonment and Orphans

More About Abandonment

Sources

More About Paternal
Abandonment and Orphans

Maternal Family Members Who Were Murdered

Name	Explained

My Relationship with Murder

____

____

____

____

____

Paternal Family Members Who Were Murdered

Name	Explained

More About Murder and Tragedy

Sources

Maternal Family Members Found in Marriage Books

Name	County/State/Year/Page

My Marriage Dates

____

____

____

____

____

Paternal Family Members Found in Marriage Books

Name	County/State/Year/Page

Rite-of-Passage

More About Maternal Marriages

More About My Marriages

Sources

More About Paternal Marriages

Sources

Maternal Family Found in Immigration Records

Name	Port/State/Year/Page

My Immigration History

Paternal Family Found in Immigration Records

Name	Port/State/Year/Page

Rite-of-Passage

More About Maternal Immigrants

More About My Citizenship

More About Paternal Immigrants

Sources

Maternal Family Members Found in Slave Records

Name	County/State/Year/Page

My Relationship with Enslavement

____

____

____

____

____

Paternal Family Members Found in Slave Records

Name	County/State/Year/Page

More About My Slavery Heritage

More About Maternal Enslavement

More About Paternal Enslavement

Sources

Maternal Family Members Found In State Historical Collections

Name	Keyword/State/Year/Page

States I Have Made History In

____

____

____

____

____

Paternal Family Members Found In State Historical Collections

Name	Keyword/State/Year/Page

Rite-of-Passage

Sources

More About Maternal Family
in State Historical Collections

More About Me in State Collections

More About Paternal Family
in State Historical Collections

Sources

Maternal Family Members Found in The National Archives (NARA) or Smithsonian Collections

Name	Collection/Link/Room

My Relationship with NARA and The Smithsonian

Paternal Family Members Found in The National Archives (NARA) or Smithsonian Collections

Name	Collection/Link/Room

More About Maternal Family
in National Collections

More About National Records and My Life

Sources

More About Paternal Family
in National Collections

Maternal Family Members Found on National Memorial Walls, Monuments and Statuary

Name	Describe/Location

My Relationship With National Monuments and Walls

____

____

____

Sources

Paternal Family Members Found on National Memorial Walls, Monuments and Statuary

Name	Describe/Location

More About Maternal Family
on Monuments and Recognition Sites

More About Me, Monuments and Recognition Sites

More About Paternal Family
on Monuments and Recognition Sites

Sources

Maternal Family Members Found
In Other Collections

Name	Type/Location

My Relationship with Other Historic Collections or Publications

Sources

Paternal Family Members Found
In Other Collections

Name	Type/Location

Rite-of-Passage

More About Maternal Family
in Other Collections

More About Me in Other Historic Collections

More About Paternal Family
in Other Collections

Maternal Family Members Found In the 1940 U. S. Census

Name	County/State/Age/Page

My Research in the 1940 Census

____

____

____

____

Paternal Family Members Found In the 1940 U. S. Census

Name	County/State/Age/Page

More About Maternal Family
in the 1940 U. S. Census

More About What I Found in the 1940 U. S. Census

More About Paternal Family
in the 1940 U. S. Census

Maternal Family Members Found
In the 1930 U. S. Census

Name	County/State/Age/Page

My Research in the 1930 Census

Paternal Family Members Found
In the 1930 U. S. Census

Name	County/State/Age/Page

More About What I Found in the 1930 U. S. Census

My Research in the 1920 Census

More About What I Found in the 1920 U. S. Census

My Research in the 1910 or 1900 U. S. Census

More About Maternal Family
in the 1910 or 1900 U. S. Census

More About What I Found in the 1910 or 1900 U. S. Census

More About Paternal Family
in the 1910 or 1900 U. S. Census

Maternal Family Members Found In the 1880 U. S. Census

Name	County/State/Age/Page

My Research in the 1880 U. S. Census

Paternal Family Members Found In the 1880 U. S. Census

Name	County/State/Age/Page

More About Maternal Family
in the 1880 U. S. Census

More About What I Found in the 1880 U. S. Census

More About Paternal Family
in the 1880 U. S. Census

Maternal Family Members Found
In the 1870 or 1860 U. S. Census

Name	County/State/Age/Page

My Research in the1870 or 1860   U. S. Census

Paternal Family Members Found
In the 1870 or 1860 U. S. Census

Name	County/State/Age/Page

More About Maternal Family
in the 1870 or 1860 U. S. Census

More About What I Found in the1870 or 1860 U. S. Census

More About Paternal Family
in the 1870 or 1860 U. S. Census

Maternal Family Members Found in Other U. S. Census

Name	County/State/Age/Page

My Research in Other U.S. Census Records

____

____

____

____

____

Paternal Family Members Found in Other U. S. Census

Name	County/State/Age/Page

More About Maternal Family
in Other U. S. Census

More About What I Found in the Other U. S. Census Records

More About Paternal Family
in Other U. S. Census

Maternal Family Members Found in Other Census Collections	
Name	Describe and Cite

My Research in Other Census Collections

Paternal Family Members Found in Other Census Collections	
Name	Describe and Cite

More About What I Found in Other Census Collections

My Current Age

Rite-of-Passage

Sources

More About Maternal Family Longest Lives

My Life Expectancy

More About Paternal Family Longest Lives

Sources

Maternal Family Members Living the Shortest Lives

Name	DOB/DOD/Cause

My Current Health Status

____

____

____

____

Paternal Family Members Living the Shortest Lives

Name	DOB/DOD/Cause

More About Maternal Family Short Lives

My Father's Life Span   -

My Mother's Life Span   -

Sources

More About Paternal Family Short Lives

134

Common Causes of Maternal Death

Name	Specify

Maternal Sources of Death Information

____

____

Paternal Sources of Death Information

____

____

Common Causes of Paternal Death

Name	Specify

Unusual Causes of Maternal Death

Mysterious Family Deaths

Sources

Unusual Causes of Paternal Death

Sources

Maternal Places of Burial

Name	Method/Location

I expect to be buried at

____

____

____

____

Paternal Places of Burial

Name	Method/Location

Rite-of-Passage

More About Maternal Family
Funerals and Burials

How I want to be Memorialized or Celebrated

Sources

More About Paternal Family
Funerals and Burials

Census of Places My Paternal Family Lived

Name	Location

Census of Places My Maternal Family Lived

Name	Location
Name	Location

Godparents in My Maternal family

Name	God Parent To

My Godparents

____

____

____

I am the Godparent to

____

____

Godparents in My Paternal family

Name	Godparent to

Sources

Rite-of-Passage

Extended Maternal Family Members

About My Current Extended Family Members

Extended Paternal Family Members

Sources

Dish Name

Ingredients

Directions

Dish Name

Ingredients

Directions

Dish Name		
Ingredients		

Directions

Dish Name		
Ingredients		

Directions

More Paternal Family Notes

I.

II.

More Maternal Family Notes

I.

II.

Paternal GREAT GREAT GRANDPARENTS

Paternal
G2 Grandfather

Paternal
G2 Grandmother

Paternal
G2 Grandfather

Paternal
G2 Grandmother

Paternal
G2 Grandfather

Paternal
G2 Grandmother

Paternal
G2 Grandfather

Paternal
G2 Grandmother

Maternal GREAT GREAT GRANDPARENTS

Maternal
G2 Grandfather

Maternal
G2 Grandmother

Maternal
G2 Grandfather

Maternal
G2 Grandmother

Maternal
G2 Grandfather

Maternal
G2 Grandmother

Maternal
G2 Grandfather

Maternal
G2 Grandmother

Catalog of Cousins

Siblings and Cousins are typically your first playmates.

Paternal 1st Cousins That I Know

Name	Mother	Father

Paternal 2nd Cousins That I Know

Name	Mother	Father

Paternal 3rd Cousins That I Know

Name	Mother	Father

Paternal 4th Cousins That I Know

Name	Mother	Father

Other Contemporary Paternal Cousins I Know "of" (But Never Met)

Name	Mother	Father

Maternal 1st Cousins That I Know

Name	Mother	Father

Maternal 2nd Cousins That I Know

Name	Mother	Father

Maternal 3rd Cousins That I Know

Name	Mother	Father

Maternal 4th Cousins That I Know

Name	Mother	Father

Other Contemporary Maternal Cousins I Know "of" (But Never Met)

Name	Mother	Father

My Branches

Children

My Biological Children	DOB	Other Parent

Adopted Children	DOB	Other Parent

Step Children	DOB	Other Parent

My Grandchildren	DOB	Parent

My Gr. Grandchildren	DOB	Parent

My Gr. Grandchildren	DOB	Parent

My G2 Grandchildren	DOB	Parent

My Step-Grandchildren	DOB	Parent

Paternal Family Lore

Documents and Sources

Adoption Records
Affidavits
Alien Register Records
Apprenticeship Records
Armed Serv. Unit Records
Artifacts
Autobiographies
Autograph Albums
Autopsies
Awards Announcements
Baby Books
Bank Statements
Baptismal Records
Bills of Sale
Biographies
Birth and Death Records
Birth Certificates
Blessing Records
Bonds
Bounty Notices
Briefs
Camera Memory
Cassettes
CD's
Checkbook Registers
Child Custody Records
Christening Records
Church Ceremonies
Church Programs
Church School Records
Clouds
Commitment Records
Conference Booklets
Confirmations
Copyrights
Credit Applications
Credit Cards
Custodial Actions
Death Certificates
Deeds
Deportment Papers
Diag. Lab Records

Diaries
Digital Video Discs
Disability Records
Discarded Cell Phones
Discharge Papers
Divorce Announcements
Divorce Decrees
Electronic Mail
Estate Sale Records
Family Archives
Family Bible Records
Family Narratives
Family Newsletters
Family Oral Histories
Film Negatives
Finance | Loan Documents
Firearms
Floppy Disc
Food Distribution Records
Genealogies
General Ledger Books
Grave Markers
Guardianship Actions
Handed-Down Effects
Hospital Records
Hotel and Lodging Records
Household Items
Immunization Records
Income Tax Records
Insurance Claims
Insurance Policies
Land Grant Records
Large Family Event Records
Letters and Post Cards
Licenses and Permits
Lineages and Pedigrees
Marriage License
Medical Records
Meeting Minutes
Meeting Proceedings
Membership Cards
Membership Records

Memoranda and Opinions
Microfilm and Forms
Military Records
Mineral Rights Records
Monuments
Mortgages
Motor Vehicle Records
Naturalization Papers
Newspapers Clippings
Notebooks
Obituaries
Passports
Patents
Pension Records
Personal Journals
Petitions to the Court
Phone Records
Photo Albums
Photographs
Picture ID Cards
Police Reports
Probate Records
Property Records
Protective Serv. Records
Quilts, Needlework, etc.
Ration Coupons
Registered Leases
Report Cards
Restraining Orders
Retirement Announcements
Reunion Announcements
Ribbons and Medals
Savings Passbooks
School Records
Scrapbooks

Selective Service Records
Separation Papers
Severance Records
Social Security Cards
Social Security Records
Stubs
Subpoenas
Summons
Tax Records
Tax Returns
Telegrams |TWX
Text Messages
Thumb Drives
Title Abstracts
Training Records
Transaction Receipts
Transcripts
Travel Itineraries
U.S. Census Records
Unemployment Records
Uniforms
Unprocessed Film
Veterans Admin. Records
Voter Cards
Warrants
Wills

Your purchase of this publication supports research in Regressive ASDs and Autism.

This publication also intends to support
2020 Development
Goals of the United Nations

Distributed through AMAZON.Com

ISBN:1720349088

$24.99 U.S.D.

Rite-of-Passage

Other Editions
of
That Fundamental Rite-of-Passage
"Self-Knowledge"

Presented by
Dalva Evette Yarrington
Information
and Data Scientist

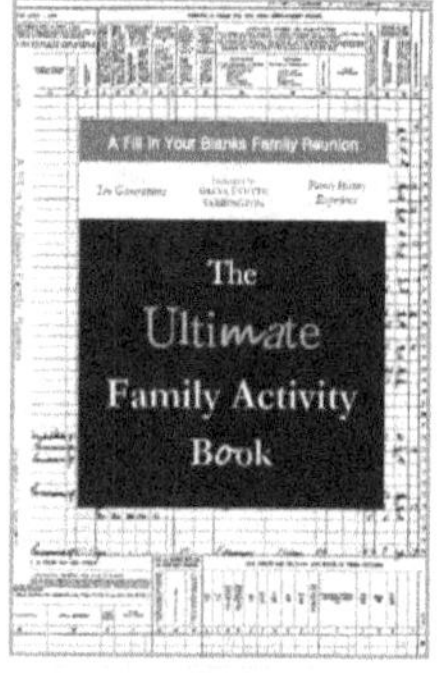

Coming
Soon...

Available on
AMAZON.Com
and from other Booksellers
Knowledge Has Power...